THE BOOK AND THE BELIEVER

ORIGINAL IN URDU BY

DR ISRAR AHMAD

TRANSLATED BY
PROF. MOHAMMAD IBRAHIM

TA-HA PUBLISHERS
LONDON

First Print 1980 Pakistan

First Published in U.K. 1988/1408
Ta-Ha Publishers Ltd
1 Wynne Rd , London SW9 0BB

Typesetting by Bookwork,
11 The Lathes, Norwich, NR2 3JD

Edited by 'AbdalHaqq Bewley

British Library Cataloguing in Publication Data

Ahmad, Israr
The Book and the Believer
1. Koran-Criticism, interpretation,etc.
I. Title
297'.1226   BP130.4

ISBN 0-907461-59-X

THE BOOK AND THE BELIEVER

CONTENTS

FOREWORD

This article, which appeared in Urdu under the title *"Musalman-o par Qur'an-i-Majid ke Huquq"*, is based on two addresses delivered by Dr Israr Ahmad to the congregations in Jamia Khazra, Samanabad, Lahore on two consecutive Fridays in January 1968 when the Muslims of Pakistan were celebrating the fourteen hundredth anniversary of the commencement of the revelation of the Holy Qur'an to the Prophet Muhammad, may the peace and blessings of Allah be upon him. During the following month, speeches on similar topics were made by Dr Ahmad at various schools and colleges in Pakistan. The subject matter of these addresses and speeches was edited and published in the Markazi Anjuman Khuddam-ul-Qur'an, Lahore.

"Musulman-o par Qur'an-i-Majid ke Huquq" is an impassioned call to the Muslims "to return to the Qur'an", to rededicate themselves to its study, and to make it the sole guide for their lives. Considering the profound purpose behind the book, I felt that it should be rendered into English both for the benefit of the English-speaking public of Pakistan and also for approaching the minds of people in other countries. Consequently I was thinking of seeking Dr Ahmad's permission to translate the book, when one day, to my delighted surprise, he himself suggested that I should translate the *Huquq*, that being the name by which the book is popularly known. Hence this translation which now appears under the title, "The Book and the Believer".

It has already been published in the form of an article by the All Pakistan Islamic Education Congress in a recent issue of their journal, "Islamic Education", under the title, "What does the Qur'an demand from its followers?", and now, thanks to their courtesy and cooperation, it is reappearing under a new title in booklet form.

I pray that it may prove helpful in the fulfilment of the great purpose which the author of the original book, Dr Israr Ahmad, has set before himself and which he is pursuing with such single-minded devotion. Amen.

MUHAMMAD IBRAHIM

2

THE QUR'AN
What it demands from every Muslim

بِسْمِ اللهِ الرَّحْمٰنِ الرَّحِيْمِ

During the last decade, international Qirat competitions have become a regular feature of the Islamic World. These competions, in which well-known reciters from different countries participate in order to display their remarkable talent for the recitation of the Qur'an, have served a number of purposes. The large audiences who have listened spell-bound to the recitation of the world-famous reciters have always been moved by the unique cadences, eloquence and grandeur of the Quran, which may have helped to strengthen their belief in its Divine origin. Moreover, these competitions have popularised *tajwid* (the art of reciting the Qur'an with correct pronunciation) in Malaysia, Indonesia and Pakistan, and Muslim children in these countries today can recite the Holy Book with a much better accent and intonation than they could possibly have done a few years ago.

Without intending to minimise the importance of reciting the Qur'an properly, it might well be asked whether these competitions have helped bridge the gulf that yawns between us and the Qur'an today and whether they have established any real connection between us and the Book of God. The answer to these questions is,"No!".

Unfortunately the great objective of establishing a real connection between us and the Qur'an has not even been achieved by the different religious seminars and symposia which have been held in Pakistan and elsewhere in recent years. The academics and scholars who have participated in the discussions at these conferences have generally dwelt on such topics as the greatness of the Qur'an, its beauties and marvels etc., but no attempt has been made to consider the fundamental questions of what our obligations are towards the Qur'an and how we can discharge these obligations.

So far as the glory and greatness of the Qur'an is concerned, we believe that it is indescribable and that its adequate comprehension is beyond the reach of the human mind. It is best known to the Lord of the heavens and the earth, Whose word it is, and to His blessed Messenger to whom it was revealed.

Therefore instead of making a presumptuous attempt to describe its unique merits, the most pertinent thing for us to undertake is to clearly

3

understand our duties and responsibilities towards the Qur'an and then to see whether or not we are conscientiously fulfilling these duties and responsibilities. If we find that we are not, we should seriously think what line of action we can adopt to enable us to do so, and then adopt it without further delay because our very salvation depends on this. Paying extravagant compliments to the Qur'an will not suffice and cannot be a substitute for actually discharging our obligations towards the Holy Book. Now what are these obligations? Or in other words, what does the Qur'an demand from us?

The Qur'an makes five demands on every Muslim. Put in simple language these demands are:
1. A Muslim is required to believe in the Qur'an.
2. He is required to read it.
3. He is required to understand it.
4. He is required to act upon its teachings.
5. He is required to convey its teaching to others.
We will now consider these demands or obligations in some detail along with a brief explanation of the terms in which they have been expressed in the Qur'an itself so that besides getting a clear idea of his duties towards the Qur'an, the reader may also become familiar with basic Qur'anic terminology.

1
IMAN WA TA'DHIM
Belief in the Divine origin of the Qur'an
and an attitude of reverence towards it

The Qur'anic term for belief in the spiritual realities is *iman* (faith) which has two phase *iqrarun bi'l-lisan* (verbal profession) and *tasdiqun bi'l-qalb* (heart-felt conviction). A verbal profession of belief in the spiritual realities upheld by Islam is the condition of a man's admittance into its fold, but true faith will emerge only when that belief deepens into a strong inward conviction.

Now what is meant by having faith in the Qur'an is firstly that one should verbally profess that the Qur'an is the Word of God which was revealed by Him through His chosen angel, Gabriel, to the last of His Messengers, Muhammad, may God shower His blessings upon him. Having made this profession a person will be accepted as a member of the Muslim community but he may not yet have attained true faith. It is only when he comes to cherish this belief with a deep inward conviction that the light of true faith will illumine his heart. When this happens he will find his heart to be full of reverence for the Holy Book. As his faith becomes stronger and stronger, his mind will come more and more under the influence of the Qur'an and his feeling of reverence for it will grow deeper and deeper. Thus faith and reverence go hand in hand.

By studying the Qur'an we learn that the first man to believe in it was the Prophet himself, closely followed by his Companions:
The Messenger believes in
what was sent down to him from his Lord,
and the believers. (2 : 28)
Their belief was a deep inward conviction that the Qur'an was *kalamu-llah* the peech of God). This conviction developed in them a reverential at it ude towards the Qur'an and created in their hearts an unbounded love and devotion for it. It was for this reason that the Holy Prophet would anxiously await the arrival of the Revelation, get impatient if it was temporarily suspended, and, when it was resumed again, memorise it with the utmost avidity and eagerness, to such an extent that Allah, out of love and affection for His Messenger, forbade him in the Book to be impatient in this regard:

**And hasten not with the Qur'an before its revelation is
accomplished unto you. (20 : 114)
Move not your tongue with it to hasten it. (75 : 16)**

Once, at an early stage in the process of Qur'anic revelation, its
continuity was interrupted for an unusually long period. It is reported
that this interruption caused the Holy Prophet so much anguish and
distress that he even thought of throwing himself down from a
mountain. So deep was his devotion to the Qur'an that he would spend
the greater part of each night in prayer and recitation, and stand reciting
the Qur'an for long hours until his feet became swollen.

His Companions were equally enamoured of the Holy Book and
would recite it for long hours at night. Many of them made a point of
going through the whole Qur'an once each week. The Holy Prophet,
though himself the recipient of the Qur'anic revelation, often asked his
Companions to recite the Qur'an to him and would be moved to tears
by the intensity of feeling aroused in his heart.

Obviously the reason why the Companions of the Holy Prophet
came to entertain such a deep love for the Qur'an in their hearts and
regarded it with so much reverence was that their belief that the Qur'an
was indeed the revealed Word of God had reached the highest stage of
certainty; a stage at which a reality is accepted as an absolute truth.

Now let us examine the condition of *our* faith in the Qur'an. We
profess that the Qur'an is a Divine revelation, and indeed we should be
thankful to the Almighty that He has included us among those who
hold this belief about His Book, but most of us are not inwardly
convinced of its being the Word of God, a revelation from the Creator
of the heavens and the earth. This is the real cause of our estrangement
from, and indifference to, the Qur'an.

Even casual introspection and self-examination will prove that our
hearts are devoid of true belief in the Qur'an and that, instead of
harbouring true faith, they have become the dwelling place of doubts
and misgivings. My fellow Muslims may resent this plain speaking on
my part but, nevertheless, it is a fact that we Muslims woefully lack
staunch faith in the Divine origin of the Qur'an. The state of doubt and
uncertainty in which we find ourselves today is described in the Qur'an
in the following words:
But those to whom the Book has been given

6

as an inheritance after them, behold,
they are in doubt about it, disquieting. (42 : 14)
This lack of faith is the reason why we neither find any reverence for
the Qur'an in our hearts, nor feel inclined to study it, nor evince any
interest in pondering over its meaning, nor think of seeking its
guidance in the conduct of our lives. As long as we do not make up this
dreadful deficiency, no useful purpose will be served by any amount of
religious instruction.

The first and foremost duty of every Muslim, therefore, is to review
his belief in the Qur'an in order to see whether his belief in the Qur'an's
being a sacred book is mere dogma on his tongue, or whether he really
is convinced of its being the Word of God which has been vouchsafed to
mankind to seek guidance from and to use as a practical code for life. If
we hold this conviction, we have reason to be thankful to Allah. If we
do not, and unfortunately the vast majority of us fall into this second
category, we should first of all make up this deficiency in our faith,
because the fulfilment of our other obligations to the Qur'an is
dependent on it.

How, then, can this deficiency be made up? The easiest and most
effective way to acquire and augment faith is to move in the society of
godly people whose own hearts are illumined by the light of true faith.
The *Sahaba* (Companions of the Holy Prophet) owed their unique faith
to the inspiring influence of their Master, who was himself the
embodiment of faith and certitude. The degree of faith which the *Sahaba*
attained on account of the physical presence of the Holy Prophet was no
longer possible after his death, but nevertheless the method of
improving and perfecting faith by keeping the company of the pious
still holds good to this day, so we should turn to the pious amongst us
for the refreshment of our faith. The pious themselves, in their turn,
find that the greatest source for the light of faith is the Qur'an. They
also make a careful study of the life of the Holy Prohet and his
Companions so that they can enjoy the intellectual and spiritual
companionship of the Messenger of Allah, may God bless him and
grant him peace, and his *Sahaba*, may God be pleased with all of them.
As far as faith in the Qur'an and its growth are concerned, we have to
depend on one source alone, and that is, of course, the Holy Qur'an
itself.

Iman (faith) is not something that can be planted in us from
outside. It is an embodiment of the fundamental truths that continually

7

flash through our inner being and are reflected by our heart. We can say that the human heart is a wonderful mirror that automatically catches and reflects the light of those universal truths that make up true faith. What happens is that sometimes the surface of this mirror gets clouded over under the effect of a bad environment or education and fails on account of this to catch and reflect the inner light of faith. To polish this mirror so that it can clearly reflect man's inner light, God, out of His benevolence to mankind, has revealed His Word to us, urging us to discern the light which exists inside ourselves and reminding us of the universal truths which in fact correspond to the intuitive perceptions of our unconscious minds.

If the Holy Book is studied and its meanings are pondered over in a genuine quest for truth, all the veils of darkness will be lifted one after the other and our inner self illumined by the light of faith. Even after the heart's mirror has been rendered capable of clearly reflecting the light of faith, we must still revert to the Qur'an whenever we find that its surface is becoming dull or obscured under the influence of worldly temptations. The following tradition, narrated on the authority of Ibn 'Umar refers to the polishing effect of the Qur'an on the mirror of the heart:

> The Holy Prophet once said, "Surely hearts get rusty just as iron gets rusty in water." He was asked how the heart's rust could be removed and he replied, "By frequent remembrance of death and recitation of the Qur'an."

The long and short of the matter is that to believe the Qur'an to be a sacred heavenly book simply as a dogma will never in itself bring about any change in our present condition or in our attitude of cold indifference towards the Holy Book. If we wish to do justice to the Qur'an and fulfil the demands it makes of us, we must first of all have the deep conviction that the Qur'an is the last and eternal message of Allah delivered to the last of His Messengers for the guidance of mankind.

As soon as we come to have this belief, our attitude towards the Qur'an will undergo a radical change. As soon as we realise that it is a revelation from our Lord, our Creator, that Most Exalted Being, the slightest apprehension of whom transcends the bounds of our limited imagination, our thinking will be completely revolutionized. When this happens we will see that the Qur'an is the greatest blessing that we possess. Its recitation will sustain our souls, and contemplation of its meanings will chasten our hearts and enlighten our minds. We shall never feel that we have studied it enough, and even after dedicating the best powers of our mind and intellect to its service and having devoted our whole lives to meditation on its meanings, we shall still feel that we have not been able to do justice to the Glorious Qur'an, the greatest of all the heavenly Books.

2

TILAWAT WA TARTIL
Slow thoughtful reading of the Qur'an with proper pronunciation

The Arabic equivalents of "reading" are *qirat* and *tilawat* . Both of these terms are used in the Qur'an in connection with its recitation. *Tilawat* is used with the meaning of reading the Qur'an with all the reverence due to it as a sacred scripture, with an open mind fully disposed to absorbing its influence, and with a keen desire to model one's life on its teaching. It is a term whose meaning is restricted to the reading of Divine revelation. *Qirat*, on the other hand, is a general term used for reading any kind of book. This distinction of meaning is borne out by the literal meanings of the two words. *Tilawat* means "to follow or walk closely behind someone", whilst *qirat* merely means "to draw or combine things together".

At first the term *qirat* was used for learning the Qur'an and acquiring its knowledge, and a *qari* was originally a scholar of the Qur'an. As time passed, however, the term gradually came to be used for reading the Qur'an with correct pronunciation and modulation according to the rules of *tajwid* . *Tilawat* came to be used as a general term for reading the sacred book with fervour and devotion for the purpose of seeking guidance and blessing from it.

Tilawat of the Holy Qur'an is not only an important form of worship but also an effective way of continually refreshing our faith. The Qur'an is not a book to be understood once and for all. It is a book to be read again and again and to be studied continually, because it provides sustenance to the human soul. Just as our earthly body is in constant need of food which is obtained from the earth, so also our soul, which is of heavenly origin, constantly needs the help of Divine revelation for fostering and strengthening itself.

If it were possible to understand the Qur'an once and for all, there would have been no need for the Holy Prophet to have read it again and again. We find, however, from studying the Qur'an itself that he was advised to do so. In the earliest days of his prophethood he was specifically instructed to stand for the greater part of the night in prayer before his Lord, reciting the Holy Book in slow rythmic tones. In the later stages of his prohetic mission, particularly when facing heavy odds and in special need of courage and fortitude to sustain himself, the prescription he received from his Lord was to recite the Qur'an:

Recite what has been revealed to thee
of the Book of thy Lord;
no man can change His words.
Apart from Him
thou wilt find no refuge.(28 : 27)

Again in the *sura* entitled *al-'Ankabut* a similar instruction is given:

Recite what has been revealed to thee of the Book,
and perform the prayer. (28 : 45)

It follows from what we have said, that constant and regular study of the Holy Qur'an is essential for providing nourishment for the soul, as a means of refreshing and reviving faith, and as a sure means of surmounting difficulties and obstacles.

The following *ayat* (Qur'anic verse) from the second *sura* of the Qur'an describes how lovers of the Qur'an manifest their love for it:

Those to whom We have given the Book,
recite it as it should be recited. (2 : 121)

May God give us the strength to be able to study the Qur'an as it should be studied. To do this we must first of all understand how the Qur'an should be recited and take the following necessary steps for the required standard of recitation to be attained.

1. TAJWID.

The first step we have to take is to acquire a thorough knowledge of the Arabic letters, their phonetic sounds, and the significance of the different kinds of pauses used in the Qur'an. The technical term used for this knowledge is *tajwid* and its acquisition is a necessity for there to be good fluent recitation. Up until the nineteen-forties almost every Muslim child in the Indian sub-continent started his education with *tajwid* so that at the very outset of their lives children were given a clear idea of the letters of the Qur'an and their correct phonetic sound.

Although as already stated at the beginning of this booklet some efforts have been made to popularise *tajwid*, the fact still remains that the vast majority of Muslim children, and even a large number of adults and old people among us, cannot read the Qur'an. This lack of ability to read even the basic text of the Qur'an is due partly to the decline of the classical system of education, which was imparted in mosques and *maktabs* to all the children of the community, rich and poor, and partly to the growing popularity of kindergartens and other types of modern primary schools, which do not include the recitation of the Qur'an in their curriculums.

I would like to suggest here, that everyone, what ever age-group they belong to, who does not possess the ability to read the Qur'an properly, should realise their deficiency and take the necessary steps to remedy it. We should also adopt it as a definite policy that the education of our children should start with *tajwid,* so that the first thing they learn will be how to recite the Qur'an properly. I may seem to be over-stressing this point, but it must be made clear that it is incumbent on every educated person to be able to recite the Qur'an with a correct accent and pronunciation, carefully observing all the necessary pauses. Without this our obligation to recite the Qur'an cannot be fulfilled.

2. DAILY RECITATION

If we wish to fulfil our obligation of reciting the Qur'an, the second thing we are required to do is to include the recitation of the Qur'an as part of our daily lives. Each one of us should recite a certain portion of the Holy Book regularly every day without fail. The portion fixed for daily recitation can vary from person to person. The maximum amount approved of by the Holy Prophet was one-third of the Qur'an. If this is done, ten *paras* (sections) are recited each day resulting in the whole Qur'an being recited in three days. A minimum portion, and anything less than this this bare minimum could not even have been imagined until very recently, might be one *para* daily so that the whole Qur'an is recited each month.

A middle way between the maximum and the minimum would be to recite the whole Qur'an once every week. This was the practice followed by the majority of the *Sahaba* and was the amount suggested to 'Abdullah b. 'Umar by the Holy Prophet. It is for this reason that the Qur'an was divided into seven sections during the time of the *Sahaba.* The first six sections consisted of three, five, seven, nine, eleven, and thirteen *suras* respectively and the seventh, known as *al-Mufassal,* comprised the rest of the Qur'an. Every section consists of approximately four *paras* and takes about two hours to recite.

12

People of a devout nature and staunch faith should do this amount of recitation daily. It does not matter whether they are learned or not, since everyone depends on the regular recitation of the Qur'an for the nourishment of their souls. To ordinary men it will serve as an admonition and remembrance of God and to the learned as a source of knowledge and reflection. Even those who ponder over the meaning of the Qur'an day and night, who think deeply over its individual *suras* for years on end, and who pause for a long time over the subtle points in its text, cannot do without this regular recitation. Indeed they require its aid all the more in the noble task they have set before themselves. Constant recitation of the Holy Book will help solve many of their problems and will continually open up new vistas of thought before their minds.

3. MELODIOUS VOICE

It is also required, for the proper recitation of the Qur'an, that a person should recite it in the best manner and the most melodious voice he can. Every human being is gifted with a love for sweet and melodious sounds and, since Islam is a natural relgion, it does not curb any of our natural tendencies but diverts them into healthy channels. As we have an instinctive love for visual and auditory beauty, we need to see the Qur'an transcribed in beautiful calligraphy and hear it recited melodiously. The Messenger of Allah urged us to *"adorn the Qur'an"* with our voices and warned us against negligence in this matter with the words:
> *"Anyone who does not recite the Qur'an in a melodious voice is not one of us."*

And he gave us the following good news as a further inducement for melodious recitation:
> *"Allah does not listen to anything so attentively as He listens to the Qur'an being recited in a sweet voice."*

It frequently happened that the Holy Prophet, while going on his way, would hear one of his Companions reciting the Qur'an in a sweet-sounding voice. He would stop and stand listening to it and then later on say how much it had pleased him. Sometimes he would ask a Companion to recite the Qur'an to him. It is related in the books of traditions that he once asked 'Abdullah b. Mas'ud to recite the Qur'an to him. The latter said:
> *"Messenger of Allah, how can I recite the Qur'an to you, when you are the one to whom it was revealed?' He replied, 'I like to hear it recited by others."*

13

'Abdullah b. Mas'ud began to recite, and as the Holy Prophet sat listening to him his eyes filled with tears which could be seen trickling down his cheeks. On another occasion he heard one of the Companions reciting in a beautiful voice which he praised by saying:

"You have been granted a share of the musical talent of the sons of David."

Although it is good to recite the Qur'an in the most melodious way possible, it is a little dangerous to over-emphasise this aspect of recitation since, if the beauty of the recitation is the result of mere show or affectation or someone makes a profession of it, it becomes a serious perversion and a reprehensible practice. However, provided that we are on our guard against this danger, there is no harm in indulging our love for the beauty of sound when reciting the Qur'an or hearing it recited in a beautiful way.

4. OUTWARD AND INWARD CONDITIONS

Reciting the Qur'an as it should be recited depends on the fulfilment of a number of outward and inward conditions. The outward conditions are that one should perform ablution before starting to recite, sit facing the *qibla*, and start the recitation with the *ta'awwudh* (seeking God's protection from Satan). Inwardly, the reciter should contemplate the greatness of the Book and the greatness of the One who revealed it and recite with complete concentration and absorbtion, with a deep feeling of submissiveness and humility, and with utmost fervour and devotion. Every reciter should read the Book of Allah with a sincere and earnest desire to reach the truth and with a firm resolve to transform himself according to its teaching. He should constantly ponder and deliberate over its meaning, not with a view of finding from it confirmation of his own concepts and theories but genuinely seeking from it the guidance it can offer.

As has been explained previously, the literal meaning of *tilawat* is "to follow or walk closely behind someone" and therefore, in its real meaning, the term demands an attitude of self-abandonment and receptivity. Such an attitude is indeed the very essence of correct *tilawat*.

5. TARTIL. Reciting in slow, measured tones.

The ideal way of reciting the Holy Book is to stand in prayer before

Allah during the last part of the night in all humility and to recite it slowly and patiently in a receptive state of mind, pausing at the proper places to enable the heart to drink in its meaning. Recitation in this way is known as *tartil* and one of the most important instructions given to the Holy Prophet in the earliest stage of his prophetic mission was to recite the Qur'an in this manner:

O you enwrapped in your robe!
Stand in prayer during the night, except for a little.
Half of it, or a little less, or a little more.
And recite the Qu'ran
in slow, measured, rythmic tones. (73 : 1-4)

This reading the Qur'an slowly and thoughtfully, making pauses at particular points in its text, resembles the way that the Qur'an was revealed in the first place. As we know, the Qur'an was not revealed all at once but descended piece by piece at intervals. In the chapter entitled *al-Furqan*, in answer to those who objected to the fact that the Qur'an was not all revealed at one time, Allah says addressing His Messenger:

(We revealed it) in this way so that we might
strengthen your heart thereby,
and we have recited it to you gradually
in slow well-arranged stages. (25 : 32)

This shows that *tartil* is an effective means of strengthening belief in the heart and there is no doubt that reading the Qur'an in this way does the utmost good to the human heart. The reciter is often moved to tears from the intensity of his experience.

In explanation of *tartil* the great scholar Abu Bakr b. 'Arabi, the author of "*Ahkamu'l-Qur'an*" quoted the following tradition on the authority of Hasan:

Once the Holy Prophet happened to pass by someone who was reciting the Qur'an. He was reciting ayat by ayat, and at the end of each ayat he would stop and weep. The Messenger of Allah, may Allah bless him and grant him peace, said to his Companions, "Have you heard God's command: Recite the Qur'an in slow, measured tones. Look! Here it is being demonstrated."

The Holy Prophet also said, instructing us about *tartil*:
"Recite the Qur'an and weep."

The Holy Prophet's own state during his night prayers is a case in point. When he stood in prayer during the night, reciting God's Book in the way we have mentioned, it is recorded that he would weep with such intensity that his breast would produce a gurgling sound like that of a kettle on the boil.

6. COMMITTING TO MEMORY

If the Qur'an is to be recited by us as it was recited by the Holy Prophet, we must learn as much of it as possible by heart. Unfortunately, the practice of memorising portions of the Book for recitation in the night prayer has all but died out. The custom of memorising the whole Qur'an does still exist but even this is losing ground. The complete memorisation of the Qur'an has been left in our society to a class of poor down-trodden people who adopt it as a profession. This did not used to be the case. In previous times this custom was common even in well-to-do families, and in some cities in pre-partition India almost every family had at least one *hafiz*. At that time it was considered discreditable for a family not to have at least one *hafiz* among its members.

There is no doubt that the memorisation of the Qur'an is a noble tradition. It forms part of the Divine dispensation for the preservation of the Qur'an and should be maintained with renewed vigour and enthusiasm. However, committing the Qur'an to memory is not within the reach of every Muslim and the point I wish to stress here is that every one of us should try his hardest to learn as much of the Qur'an as possible by heart, in order to be able to recite it standing before his Lord in prayer. This is, in fact, an essential pre-requisite for reciting the Book of God in the way it should be recited and as it was recited by the Holy Prophet himself but unfortunately, we seem to have lost our eagerness and fervour for doing it.

Even the men of religious learning among us have grown negligent about this matter and those who lead the public prayers in the mosques are, unfortunately, not much better. Most of them seem to be satisfied with a few short *suras* they committed to memory in their youth and go on repeating them in the prayer again and again. Surely this is a sad state of affairs which must be changed. All of us should develop in our hearts a deep love for the Qur'an and look upon any part of the Book we have memorised as our most real and valuable asset, taking every opportunity to increase and enhance it. In this way we will be able to enjoy the blissful joy of true *tartil* and provide for our souls a greater and greater amount of sustenance in the best possible form.

16

3
TADHAKKUR WA TADABBUR
Recalling through the Qur'an the fundamental truths intuitively recognised by human nature and reflecting on its meaning

We have considered two of the claims that the Qur'an has on us - that we should believe in it and that we should recite it. Now we will look at the third claim it has on us which is that we should understand it. Obviously the Qur'an was revealed to be understood. There would be no sense in believing in it if we could not follow its meaning, and how could it serve as a source of guidance for us if we were unable to comprehend its message. Recitation without understanding is excusable in the case of people who have not been fortunate enough to receive any education and even clumsy recitation on their part may be acceptable and gain them a reward and blessings from God.

However, if people who have devoted a considerable part of their lives to their own education, and may even have learnt a langage apart from their own, recite the Qur'an thoughtlessly and without understanding its meaning, their recitation will be totally futile and fruitless. Moreover, it is quite possible that with their heedless recitation these ignorant people may be guilty of making a mockery of recitation or even, God forbid, of holding the Qur'an itself up to ridicule. But if these people make a firm resolve to acquire knowledge of the Qur'an and set out in earnest to do so, there is no harm in their continuing to recite the Qur'an in the best way that they can and in this case it is probable that their recitation, even without understanding, will be acceptable to God and earn them a reward.

As for the comprehension of the Qur'an , it is not a simple matter. It has numerous stages and grades, accessible to different people according to the degree of their understanding. The Holy Qur'an is like a boundless ocean from which a scholar can bring out pearls of knowledge according to his natural ability, mental make-up, and intellectual capacity. His efforts to understand the Qur'an will be rewarded according to the enthusiasm, time and labour that he puts into its study and research.

It will be found at the same time that, so far as its comprehension is concerned, nobody, however intelligent and learned they may be, will ever feel that he has done true justice to the Qur'an even though he may have spent his whole life poring over its pages and meditating over its meaning. The Holy Prophet himself described the the Qur'an as a treasure which would never be exhausted, and the nature of its guidance is such that we will never cease to be in need of reverting to it and reflecting on it. Therefore let men of courage and determination come forward to undertake the tremendous task of studying the Qur'an, fired with the noble ambition of surpassing others in this field.

We are urged again and again in the Qur'an to study it intelligently, bringing our thought to bear upon it, and exercising our reasoning faculty in following its arguments and comprehending its meaning. To this end, it uses such terms as *fahm, 'aql, fiqh,* and *fikr,* but another important term, more widely used in the Qur'an in this connection, is *tadhakkur.* To understand the significance of this term we have to note that the Qur'an frequently calls itself *dhikr, dhikra* and *tadhkira.* *Tadhakkur* pertains to the first stage in comprehension of the Qur'an and indicates the real purpose it should serve. It also alludes to the fact that the Qur'anic teaching is not extraneous to human nature. It indicates that the Qur'an actually reflects the experience of man's inner self and is meant to awaken reminiscences of something already apprehended rather than impart anything absolutely new.

The Holy Qur'an appeals to all thoughtful people whom it addresses as *ulu'l-albab* (men of understanding) and *qawmun ya'qilun* (people who understand), asking them to reflect and ponder over the outer material universe as well as the inner universe of the spirit, since both are replete with signs (*ayats*) of their Almighty Creator. Simultaneously it invites them to deliberate over its own signs (*ayats*), the Divinely inspired verses of which it is comprised. In the chapter entitled *Yunus,* it says:

Thus do we explain the signs in detail
for a people who reflect. (10 : 24)
In the chapter entitled *an-Nahl* it says:
We have sent down to you the Remembrance
that you may make clear to mankind
what was sent down to them; and so that haply
they might reflect. (16 : 44)

Again in the same vein in the second chapter, *al- Baqara:*

So God makes clear His signs to you,
that haply you will understand. (2 : 242)

Reflecting on the three categories of signs - the signs in the Qur'an, the signs in the physical universe and the signs in the spiritual world of the human heart - a man will be able to perceive a perfect concord between them and, with the realisation of this concord, he will grasp certain fundamental truths which are borne out by the internal testimony of his own nature. In other words truths hidden within his inner self will emerge from its depths and shine in all their brilliance on the screen of his consciousness. Full and intense awareness of the Absolute Reality, which forms the core of true faith, will then spring into his conscious mind just as the memory of a forgotten thing shoots up from the dark depths of the mind to its surface at the prompting of a pertinent suggestion. It is for this phenomenon that the Qur'an uses the term *tadhakkur*.

Every-one, whatever their intellectual capacity , is in constant need of *tadhakkur* in order to recall to the mind truths that have been forgotten and to keep in mind truths that are likely to be forgotten. Because of this God has made the Qur'an an easy means of *tadhakkur* - a fact which is stated four times in a single *sura* :
Now We have made the Qur'an easy for reminding(dhikr).
Is there any that will be reminded? (54)

The Qur'an therefore makes it unequivocally clear that the benefits of *tadhakkur* can be gained from it by everybody. It does not matter if a person's intelligence is limited, or his knowledge of logic and philosophy poor, or that he has no fine sense of language and literature, for *tadhakkur* is gained from the Qur'an by having a noble heart, a sound mind, and an untainted nature not perverted by any kind of crookedness. Such people should go on reciting the Qur'an, understanding its simple meaning which is all that is required for the purposes of *tadhakkur*.

The Quran has been made easy in different ways for those who are striving to understand it and derive *tadhakkur* from it. Firstly, its central theme and basic subject matter are neither new nor unfamiliar to human nature. When reading the Qur'an you often feel that you are listening to the echoes of your own inner self. Secondly, the mode of inference adopted is simple and natural, and difficult or abstruse subjects are made clear by means of straightforward parables. Thirdly, although

19

the Qur'an, is a masterpiece of literature and an example of unsurpassable eloquence, yet its language is generally simple and anyone with a basic grasp of Arabic can easily understand it with the exception of a few difficult parts.

However, a basic knowledge of Arabic is essential for gaining *tadhakkur* from the Qur'an. Looking at a translation at the same time as reciting the Qur'anic text in Arabic is not sufficient. I honestly feel that it is imperative for every Muslim to learn enough Arabic to enable him to understand the meaning of the Qur'anic text as he reads along without having to continually consult a translation.

On the Day of Judgment when they are face-to-face with the Almighty, I cannot see what possible excuse in their own defence those who are not only educated but have obtained graduate and post-graduate degrees are going to be able to put forward. How are they going to be able to explain to their Lord the fact that they had time to master such difficult arts and sciences as medicine and engineering but were not able to spare enough time to learn even the small amount of Arabic that would have enabled them to follow the meaning of His Book. Out of a sincere regard and genuine concern for these Muslims, let me assert that their negligence in the matter of learning Arabic is tantamount to not only ridiculing the Book of Allah but also treating it with contempt, and they should realise that by their irresponsible behaviour in this regard they are rendering themselves liable to an awful chastisement and a dreadful penalty.

In my opinion to learn as much Arabic as will enable a person to follow the meaning of the Qur'an is a duty that every educated Muslim owes to the Qur'an, and not to fulfil this duty is to be unjust both to the Qur'an and ourselves.

The second stage in the comprehension of the Qur'an is *tadabbur fi'l-Qur'an* which means reflecting on it deeply, making it a subject of intense study, and diving into the depths of its knowledge and wisdom. The Qur'an requires such deep study because it is *hudan li'n-nas* (guidance for people). Not only does it guide the common people by presenting them with a correct view of God and the universe as well as sound moral principles, but it also contains perfect guidance for men of learning and understanding and has always served them as a beacon of light in every intellectual and spiritual crisis in their lives.

This need to ponder and reflect on the Qur'an is something which is emphasised within the text of the Qur'an itself:

A book We have sent down to you, full of blessings, that men of understanding may ponder its signs,

and so remember. (38 : 29)

In another place it says in a mildly admonishing vein:

What, do they not ponder the Qur'an? (4 : 82)

And again:

What do they not ponder the Qur'an?
Or is it that there are locks upon their hearts? (47 : 24)

Just as the Qur'an is easy for *tadhakkur* so it is correspondingly difficult for *tadabbur*. Those who dive into this boundless ocean know that it is not possible to fathom its depth. We learn from authentic traditions that the Companions of the Holy Prophet used to ponder over the different *suras* of the Qur'an for years on end. It is reported about 'Abdullah b. 'Umar that he spent eight years contemplating *al-Baqara*, the second chapter of the Qur'an. Let it be noted that this was the case with people who spoke the same language in which the Qur'an had been revealed and who, being the contemporaries of the Holy Prophet, had seen it being revealed before their own eyes. It was not necessary for them to learn the Arabic language or its grammar, or to undertake research for ascertaining the historical background of different *ayats* or *suras* and the occasions on which they were revealed, for they already knew these things. But in spite of having these immense advantages, they still spent years pondering over each *sura*.

This shows that diving into this sea of knowledge and wisdom is no easy task and that in fact it calls for strenuous labour and constant application. In later ages great scholars like Tabari, Zamakhshari, Razi, and many others of the same calibre dedicated their whole lives to the study of the Qur'an, but none of them was able to study more than a single aspect of the Book, and they all failed to do justice even to the one aspect they concentrated on. Throughout the fourteen centuries since its revelation there has been no scholar, however voluminous his work, who can claim to have said all that can be said about the Qur'an and to have left no room for further deliberation.

In his *Ihya 'Ulumi'd-Din,* Imam al-Ghazali quotes the words of one of the great scholars which bring out the difference between the ordinary recitation of the Qur'an for the purposes of *tadhakkur* and its thoughtful study for the purposes of *tadabbur:* "There is a recitation which takes me a week to finish the Qur'an. There is another kind of recitation which takes me a month and yet another which takes me a year. There is yet another kind of recitation which I started thirty years ago but which I have still not been able to complete.

The qualifications needed for deliberative study of the Qur'an are extremely hard to acquire and it is not possible for a man to attain these qualifications unless he devotes himself to it solely and wholly, and makes the learning and teaching of the Qur'an the be-all-and-end-all of his life. For such a study a man requires not only a thorough knowledge of the Arabic language and its grammar, but also a refined literary taste to appreciate the beauty, force and eloquence of the Qur'anic language. He must acquire a good grounding in the actual language in which the Qur'an was revealed by making a critical study of the works of the pre-Islamic poets and orators. Then there are the terms and modes of expression evolved by the Qur'an itself. A clear understanding of these is also a necessary part of the mental equipment of a student of the Qur'an. He should also be able to appreciate the co-ordination and coherence of the Qur'an. He must grasp the deep significance of the present order of the *suras* in the Qur'an, which is different from the chronological order in which they were revealed. He must also comprehend the sequence of thought between one *sura* and another as well as between the verses of the same *sura.*

All this represents an extremely arduous task which has defied the patience of all but the most determined scholars but, however difficult it is, it has to be accomplished if the Qur'an is to be properly understood. In fact, it is only when diving into the Qur'an to grasp the subtle sequence between its different parts that it is possible to form an idea of the unfathomable depths of this boundless sea and bring out from it the finest pearls of knowledge and wisdom.

Besides the branches of learning referred to above, a good knowledge of *hadith* and the previous scriptures is also necessary for understanding the Qur'an, and together, all the things we have mentioned, make up the complete background of classical knowledge which should be possessed by a truly qualified student of the Qur'an. But this is not all.

Even with all this, a man is not yet equipped to undertake *tadabbur*. He still has to reckon with the modern sciences. We know that experimental and theoretical sciences are not static and that their level of development has been different at different times. A scholar who wants to undertake the momentous task of comprehending the Qu'ran should also have an understanding of modern sciences - physical, biological and social. He should be conversant with the fundamental hypotheses of the different sciences and with the methods of deduction and inference employed by each. He should also keep himself in touch with the latest trends and achievements in every important field of human inquiry. This knowledge of modern arts and sciences is essential for him as it will widen his mental outlook and increase his intellectual capacity.

Thus equipped he will be able to embark upon his great enterprise. The Qur'an is a boundless ocean on which the sailor can only sail as far as his limited capacity will take him; and what useful discoveries he makes on his journey will depend on the guidance he receives and the range of his knowledge and the breadth of his vision.

It is particularly necessary for the dissemination of the Qur'an and the propagation of its message in the present-day world - also a duty incumbent on every Muslim - that the Qur'anic scholar should be fully equipped with modern knowledge. Otherwise he will be unable to discharge this duty. Each generation inherits a large amount of knowledge from its predecessors and transmits it on to the succeeding generation with its own contribution added to it. Thus knowledge goes on accumulating as it passes from one generation to the next.

By this process of transmission, the present generation has received a stupendous stock of knowledge in the fields of logic and philosophy, religion and metaphysics, ethics and psychology, and other social sciences. The huge amount of current knowledge has dominated people's minds and they have developed a naive belief in many wrong views. We require a fairly good knowledge of modern sciences and should be conversant with not only their subject matter but also with their original sources and the system of principles underlying them. Only then will it be possible to deal a crushing blow, in the manner of Ibn Taimiyya and Ghazali, at the very root of the false notions prevailing in our time.

In some respects, the present age can be considered to have touched the highest watermark. Besides the remarkable developments in the field of social sciences it has witnessed an unprecedented advance in the physical sciences and technology which has stunned the human mind and rendered it incapable of making a critical appraisal of the misguided and misleading views that have found currency in the modern world.

Under these circumstances, the imperative duty of comprehending and interpreting the Qur'an cannot be accomplished unless some patient and persevering men address themselves to this momentous task with single-minded devotion, equipping themselves with both the classical and modern knowledge necessary for it. These dedicated and fully equipped scholars of the Qur'an would carry out a searching analysis of modern knowledge and sift the sound from the fallacious in the light of the Qur'an. They would approach the intellect of modern man making judicious use of modern terminology and sophisticated methods of logical reasoning. In this way they would be able to illuminate the minds of their contemporaries with the light of Qur'anic guidance and in this way the duty of "explaining the Qur'an to the people", performed by the Holy Prophet himself during his own life-time, would be fulfilled by his community in the present age.

Now the question arises of how to produce such scholars. Obviously they cannot be produced until we have, all over the Islamic world, a network of universities which concentrate on Qur'anic research and make it the hub of their intellectual activity. Round this central department, these universities should build up other departments like a department of theoretical sciences which would include logic, metaphysics, ethics, psychology and religion; a department of social sciences to include economics, politics and law; and a department of physical sciences such as mathematics, chemistry, physics, geology and astronomy. Every student who joined such a university would take Qur'anic studies as a compulsory subject and one or more of the other disciplines as elective subjects according to his own taste and aptitude. This would enable him to carry out research on the Qur'an within the sphere of his own specialist field of study and thus present the light and guidance of the Qur'an effectively to people.

Clearly this is no easy task, which is why it is not the responsibilty of every person. It should be undertaken only by those people who are born with an unquenchable thirst for knowledge and whose minds are agitated by obstinate problems which can only be solved through prolonged thinking and reasoning. Such men are compelled to seek knowledge in the same way as a starving person is compelled to seek food and drink. They constantly utter the prayer, "O Lord, increase me in knowledge." If these men manage to receive correct guidance they generally gain a good share of knowledge and wisdom.

Real comprehension and interpretation of the Qur'an is the province of such students as these, but, of course, every seeker of knowledge can participate in this noble task according to his ability and the time he can devote to it. To encourage people to study the Qur'an, the Prophet said:
> *"The best among you are those who learn the Qur'an and teach it to others."*

In the same vein, we have the general instruction in the Qur'an:

It is not for all the believers to go forth together;
but why should not a party of them
from every group withdraw themselves
to develop an understanding of religion so they can warn
their people when they return to them. (9 : 122)

This understanding of religion is the fruit of a deep and meditative study of the Qur'an and it is what the Holy Prophet wanted his Companions to develop. He made a special prayer for some of them to be granted a keen insight into matters pertaining to religion and his observation:
> *"The best of you in the time before Islam are the best of you in Islam,"*

was conditional to their having acquired this insight.

4

HUKM WA IQAMA
Moulding the personal life of the individual and the corporate life of the community according to the teachings of the Qur'an

We have already considered three of the duties we owe to the Qur'an and now we proceed to consider the fourth which is that we should act on its teachings. It is obvious that the reason that we are required to believe in the Qur'an, study it and ponder over its meaning is in order for us put its teachings into practice in our daily lives. The Qur'an is not a book of magical formulas or mantras to be chanted to ward off evil, nor is it merely a means of obtaining blessing. Its verses are not to be recited only for the sake of getting a reward from God or reducing the agony of death. Nor is it an object of investigation and research in the sense of merely providing good exercise for our intellectual and imaginative faculties to enable us to indulge in all sorts of abstruse thinking and useless hair-splitting when interpreting its meaning.

The Qur'an, as we know, is *hudan li'n-nas* (guidance for mankind). The purpose for which it was revealed will only be realised if people act upon its teachings and actually make it their guide in every sphere of their lives. The Holy Prophet made it abundantly clear that reciting the Qur'an and pondering over its meaning will serve no useful purpose if we do not try to mould our lives according to its injunctions. If we disregard what it says, our recitation, far from doing us any good, will actually undermine our faith. In this context the Qur'an speaks in the following unequivocal terms:

> **Whosoever does not conduct affairs**
> **according to what Allah has sent down,**
> **they are unbelievers. (5 : 44)**

This point is further clarified and emphasised by the following traditions of the Holy Prophet:

> *"None of you is a believer until all his desires are in accordance with what I have brought."*

and also:

> *"Anyone who holds to be lawful what the Qur'an declares unlawful is not a believer in the Qur'an."*

No-one will obtain any real benefit from the Qur'an, unless he studies it with a firm resolution to abide by its injunctions and modify his character according to its teaching, however heavy the odds or great the sacrifice involved. As we have already stated when explaining the literal meaning of the term *tilawat,* the Qur'an yields its perfect guidance only to those who abandon themselves to it and pore over it long and assiduously. It is only self-abandonment combined with prolonged concentration that can generate the state of submissiveness and self-effacement alluded to in the above *hadiths.* Anyone desiring to get the full benefit of Qur'anic guidance must first put himself into this state of mind. Then, as his contact with the Qur'an becomes closer and closer, he will gain greater and greater enlightenment from it:

But those who are guided,

He increases them in guidance,

and grants them true fear of Him. (47 : 1)

In other words, if a person actually starts to move forwards under the guidance of the Qur'an, he will soon find himself marching steadily along the straight path and will go on gradually rising to higher and higher planes of spiritual development.

If, on the other hand, a person has not made up his mind to transform himself in accordance with Qur'anic teaching, any time he spends reciting the Holy Book will simply be wasted. Recitation of the Qur'an, rather than doing him any spiritual good, may actually prove to be a curse for him. Imam al-Ghazali quotes one of the mystics as saying: 'Some people who recite the Qur'an get nothing from it except the imprecations in it. If someone recites, "God's curse is on the liars," when he himself is a liar, he becomes the target of the curse.' In the same way, if someone recites:

But if you do not (give up practising usury)

then take notice of war

from Allah and His messenger. (2 : 279)

when he himself is violating this injunction of God Almighty, he becomes the person addressed by the *ayat.* It is the same with those who give short measure or short weight and those who indulge in slander and backbiting when they recite respectively:

Woe to the stinters... (83 : 1)

and

Woe to every backbiter, slanderer... (104 : 1)

They will find that these dreadful warnings are meant for them. From all this it is clear what people gain from recitation of the Qur'an when their actions are not in accordance with its teaching.

As for those who study the Qur'an in order to investigate it, reflect on its meanings, and write books about it, but do not put its injunctions into practice, we can state that they are without doubt the worst kind of sinners. Their study and research is nothing more than indulgence in a fascinating intellectual exercise in which they play with the Holy Book or even make fun of it. Consequently, instead of guiding them to the right path, the Qur'an causes them to go astray:

By it He leads many astray
and by it He guides many to the right path. (2 : 26)

These so-called Qur'anic scholars disseminate all sorts of mischievous interpretations and become instrumental in misleading and misguiding people in various ways. Their whole approach to the Holy Book is motivated by a vicious attempt to pursue the abstruse and the recondite. The Qur'an has aptly described their motives in taking this course of action in the following words:

They follow the ambiguous parts, seeking discord,
and seeking its esoteric interpretation. (3 : 7)

The *Sahaba* understood the supreme importance of embodying the teachings of the Qur'an in their lives. That is the reason why those who had a special aptitude for understanding the Qur'an and who might spend years pondering over a single *sura* , would make such long pauses in their study. They would not continue until they were satisfied that they had put into practice what they had already learned. The reader may be surprised to know that when the Companions talked of learning a *sura* by heart they did not just mean preserving it in their memory but also comprehending its meaning clearly and moulding their behaviour in the light of the guidance they had received from it. In other words, what was originally meant by the phrase *hifdhu'l-Qur'an,* which has now come to mean merely memorising the Arabic text of the Qur'an, was that its words should be preserved in the memory, its knowledge treasured up in the mind, and its teachings reflected in behaviour, so that the whole personality was imbued with the spirit of the Qur'an and the deepest recesses of the being illumined by its light.

The relationship between daily life and the Qur'an, which was visible in the conduct of the Companions, found its consumate and perfect expression in the life of the Holy Prophet. His wife A'isha, whose intimate knowledge of his life destined her for the role of one of the major teachers of the Muslim community, was once questioned concerning the Prophet's character. She replied that his character was the

Qur'an. This extremely wise and judicious answer brings into relief the deep impact that the Qur'an has on the life of the true Muslim.

In short, the best way to benefit ourselves from the study of the Qur'an is to go on mending our ways and modifying our behaviour in the light of its teachings while at the same time developing a deeper and deeper understanding of its meanings so that the Qur'an comes to permeate our characters. Otherwise there is a danger, in the light of the Prophet's statement that the Qur'an is clear argument either for us or against us, that our knowledge and understanding of the Qur'an may prove an irrefutable argument against us and become instrumental in bringing upon us a greater punishment from the Almighty on account of our negligence and indifference.

At this point it is necessary to explain that 'amal bi'l-Qur'an (acting according to the injunctions of the Qur'an) has two phases - individual and collective. There are injunctions which apply to a person's individual or private life which can be put into practice straight away and which become binding on him the moment he learns of them. There can be no justification for any postponement or delay in carrying out these injunctions and the punishment for failing to do so appears in the form of a withdrawal of Divine grace, the result of which is failure to live up to the principles embodied in the Qur'an. The disparity between a person's words and deeds, between his belief and his actions, which is so hateful to God, results in hypocrisy, and this is referred to by the Prophet in his words:

"*Most of the hypocrites among my people will be readers of the Qur'an.*"

Therefore, the only safe course to follow is to begin to act immediately on what you learn from the Qur'an, for hypocrisy is the most severely punished of all wrong-actions.

As for those injunctions which pertain to the affairs of collective social life and which are beyond the control of one individual, it is clear that we are not obliged to implement them immediately. Nevertheless, it is our duty to try as far as possible to change the existing conditions and construct a society based on Qur'anic principles so that it may become possible to act upon the entire teaching of the Qur'an. In these circumstances, the efforts made by a person towards this end will be **"an excuse for him with his Lord"** and will be accepted as a substitute for complete compliance with all the injunctions themselves.

29

However, if he does not make any effort in this direction and remains content with the discharge of his ordinary domestic obligations like the bringing-up of his children, etc., then even his enactment of personal and private injunctions will resemble the reprehensible practice of those who are censured by the Qur'an in the following *ayat*:

What, do you believe in part of the Book
and disbelieve in part (2 : 85)

Just as *tadhakkur* is a general term for the understanding of the Qur'an, similarly the most general and widely-used term for acting in accordance with its teaching is *hukm bima anzala'llah* (making decisions in the light of what Allah has revealed). For grasping the real significance of the word *hukm*, which lies at the core of this term we should consider its use in the following *ayats*:

(i) Surely authority belongs to God alone. (12: 4)
Here *hukm* has been used in the sense of "command" or "authority".

(ii) Thus have We revealed it to you
to be a criterion for judgment, in Arabic.. (13: 37)
Here the Qur'an has been styled as *hukm*, which has been translated here as "a criterion for judgment".

(iii) We have sent down to you the Book in truth,
that you may judge between men
according to what Allah has shown you. (4:108)
Here a derivative of the word *hukm* has been used to indicate the mission of the Holy Prophet.

(iv) *Ayats* 47-49 of *sura* five which categorically state that those who do not judge by the light of the Qur'an are none other than the unbelievers, the wrong-doers, and the rebellious.

If You punish them, they are Your servants.
If You forgive them,
You are the Exalted, the Wise. (5:121)

How aptly the following *hadith* of the Holy Prophet applies to our present situation:

"Indeed, God exalts some with this Book and by it He disgraces others."

The *Sahaba* attained power and glory by acting in accordance with the teachings of the Qur'an while we have fallen into an abyss of degradation because we have forsaken it.

If one tried to express the sense of the word *hukm* in a single word,

30

the nearest English equivalent would be "judgment" or "decision", but in order to fully understand its significance we must reflect on the two basic constituents of a person's conduct - thought and action. When a view-point or attitude of mind so completely dominates a person that it becomes the thing that determines his judgments and decisions, then what he does will be automatically subordinated to it. The Qur'an uses the term *hukm bima anzala'llah* (deciding every issue in the light what Allah has revealed) rather than *'amal bi'l-Qur'an* (acting according to the Qur'an) to make it clear that a person is only considered to be acting according to the Qur'an when his whole thinking is completely dominated by it and the knowledge of reality imparted to him by it has penetrated deep down into his mind and heart.

Another term used by the Qur'an to denote the idea of acting upon the teaching contained in it is *iqama* (standing fast by). Referring to the Jews and Christians, it says:

If only they had stood fast by the Torah and the Gospel
and all that was revealed to them from their Lord,
they would have enjoyed abundance
from above and beneath. (5 : 66)

Again it is used in *ayat* 71 of the same *sura*, which makes this pronouncement:

Say: 'O People of the Book,
you have nothing to stand on
until you stand fast by the Torah and the Gospel and
what has been revealed to you from your Lord. (5 : 71)

Hukm bima anzala'llah (deciding every issue in the light of what Allah has revealed) pertains to making the conduct of the individual conform to the teaching of the Qur'an, whereas *iqamatu ma unzila mina'llah* (standing fast by what has been revealed from Allah) pertains to the collective life of the community. It signifies the establishment of a system of life, based on perfect social justice, which ensures balance and harmony between the individual members of society and society as a whole. When people come to owe allegiance to such a perfect social order, the possibility of tyranny, transgression, cruelty and injustice is absolutely ruled out and all the doors of political oppression and economic exploitation are closed. This is why, in the first *ayat* quoted above, well-being and prosperity are referred to as an inevitable concomitant of such a system. The establishment of a perfectly just and equitable social order is precisely the reason that God deputed His Messengers and sent down His Books:

**Indeed We sent Our Messengers with the clear signs,
and We sent down with them the Book and the Balance
so that men might establish justice. (57 : 25)**

In the second section of the chapter entitled *ash-Shuraa,* we have a detailed discussion on this topic. Here we are given a clear picture of the co-ordination which exists between the fundamental concepts of Islam and this co-ordination is mentioned in a very meaningful and judicious sequence. First comes *hukmi'llahi* (God's authority or decision); then *iqamati'd-din* (establishment of the religion); next *iman bi'l-kitab* (belief in the Book); and finally *qiyami nizami 'adli'l-'ijtima-iyya* (creation of a just and equitable social order).

To begin with, we have the fundamental principle that God's authority and decision reign supreme, and in *ayat* 10, we are accordingly directed to recognise and uphold it in all circumstances:

**Whatever thing about which you disagree,
the decision in it rests with God. (42 : 10)**

Ayat 13 refers to the manifestation of God's authority or decision in the form of *din* (religion) and *shari'ah* (law).

**He has established for you
the same religion that He enjoined on Noah -
which We have revealed to you -
and that which We enjoined on
Abraham, Moses and Jesus:
that you should remain steadfast in religion,
and not become divided about it. (42 : 13)**

Then in *ayat* 15, the Holy Prophet is instructed to declare his belief in the Book and work for the creation of a just society by dispensing justice to the people:

**And so call them and go straight
as you have been commanded;
and do not follow their caprices.
Say: 'I believe in the Books that God has sent down,
and I have been commanded
to judge justly between you. (42 : 15)**

This whole discussion is summed up in *ayat* 17:

**It is God who has sent down the Book in truth,
and the Balance.
What will make you realise
that the Hour may be close at hand? (42 : 17)**

32

Here, as in the *ayat* from *al-Hadid* above, we have the word *mizan* (balance) which is a very significant term and is used in several different places in the Qur'an. Maulana Shabbir Ahmad 'Uthmani has offered a comprehensive explanation of the term in the following words: 'God has guided man to devise the material "balance" by which material objects are weighed. He has also granted man intellectual "balance" which is another name for sound common sense; and also moral "balance" which is another name for the sense of justice and fair play; but the most important "balance" granted to us is the Religion of Truth which settles the basic issue of the respective rights of the Creator and His creatures and by which all issues can be justly decided.'

According to the Qur'an, the real reason for the deviation of people from the true religion, and the chaos and anarchy in the world, is their wicked tendency to dominate other people and keep them in subjugation. In *ayat* 14 of this same *sura* where the Muslims are exhorted to curb schismatic trends, the basic cause leading to people breaking away from the Religion of God and establishing sects has been pointed out:

> **And they only split up**
> **after knowledge had come to them,**
> **through iniquity and oppression**
> **among themselves. (42: 14)**

We are now led to consider the final result of moulding our thoughts and actions on the teachings of the Qur'an. As we have stated above, the result should be the establishment of God's sovereignty and the rule of justice in the world. When such an order is set up, the world is freed of every kind of iniquity and oppression. Then priests and divines cannot install themselves as godheads; the wealthy can no longer confine the circulation of wealth to themelves and there is no possibility of any kind of coercion and exploitation. All become servants of Allah and begin to behave towards one another as brothers. The rulers consider it their primary duty to safeguard the rights of the weak at any cost, and not to allow the powerful to tyrannise them in any way.

The establishment of such a just and equitable order in accordance with the teaching of the Qur'an is the bounden duty of all Muslims. Its fulfilment is their collective responsibility for which they will be answerable to the Almighty. It is, therefore, time that they clearly understood this responsibility and set about discharging it. That could be why, at the end of the discussion in *sura* 42 we have been talking about, there is a mention of the imminence of the Day of Judgment. It says:

Perhaps the Hour is at hand. (42 : 17)

This implies the warning that we should not be guilty of any negligence or delay in this matter lest we be suddenly overtaken by the Last Day. This duty which we owe to the Book of God will only be fulfilled if we actually set up a system of social justice, **'so that people may establish justice'** and their rulers **'may judge justly between them'**. We shall find that we possess the foundation and structure of this system in the fundamental principles of our religion and its code of laws that have all been articulated in the Qur'an.

It may well be asked what the practical measures that should be taken in order to fulfil this duty are? Although a comprehensive answer to this question is beyond the scope of this booklet, a few remarks on this topic will not be out of place. Firstly, it should be understood that the implementation of the fundamental principles of religion in society and the establishment of the just and equitable order envisaged by the Qur'an should not be conceived along the lines of a social, economic or political movement; nor should we strive for the obtainment of this splendid ideal as we do for the success of these kind of movements. Such a course of action would be fraught with grave danger and could even prove suicidal. We must know that just as there is only one method to bring about the transformation of an individual as required by Islam, so there is only one method of carrying out an Islamic revolution in society.

As far as the individual is concerned, we should first make the Qur'an dominate his heart and mind so that his emotions, thoughts, and reasoning, function in harmony with its spirit and then his actions will necessarily be in harmony with its teachings. It is the same with the change in society demanded by Islam. We first have to illumine the minds and hearts of the intelligentsia with the light of the Qur'an so that they are intellectually and spiritually transformed. After the intelligentsia, who are the brain of the community, have been instructed, the light of the Qur'an can easily be spread to other people who are the limbs of the community which follow the dictates of the brain. Thus the heart of the entire community will beat in unison with the teachings of the Qur'an and the fundamental principles of God's religion will function in the form of a perfect system of collective justice.

There is no other way of bringing about this revolution. The plea that this goal can be achieved by launching a political movement through the exploitation of the emotional attachment which a Muslim people has to its hereditary religion is absolutely without foundation, and making such an attempt would be like building on sand.

Hoping to be excused for this digression, I must repeat that the duty of acting upon the teachings of the Qur'an, which has two aspects, *hukm bima anzala'llah* and *iqamatu ma unzila mina'llah,* is an absolute imperative upon the Muslims both individually and collectively. Therefore each of us must earnestly endeavour to discharge this great responsibility according to his means and capacity.

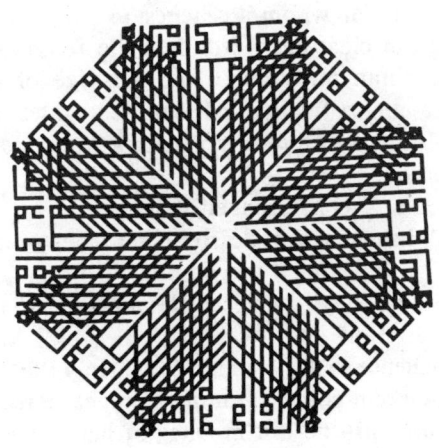

5
TABLIGH WA TABYIN
Propagation of the Qur'anic message and its exposition

Along with the four duties owed to the Qur'an which we have
already outlined, there is a further duty which devolves on every
Muslim and which must be discharged according to individual strength
and ability. This is the communication of its teaching to others. For
"communicating the message of the Qur'an to the people", the most
appropriate and comprehensive term is *tabligh*. It has several forms and
grades. Teaching the Qur'an to others is one form of *tabligh*.
Explaining its meaning to people is another higher form of *tabligh*.

In order to understand the importance of this duty, let us consider
the purpose for which the Qur'an was revealed. This purpose is stated
by the Qur'an itself in the following words:

This is a message to be conveyed to all human beings,
that they may be warned by it. (14 : 52)

Again the Holy Prophet is commanded in the Qur'an to say concerning
the objective of the revelation:

This Qur'an has been revealed to me
that I may warn you thereby,
and all whom it reaches. (6 : 19)

It also announces in clear-cut words that the foremost duty of the
Prophet was the communication of the message of the Qur'an to
mankind with the utmost fidelity and that the slightest negligence on
his part in the fulfilment of this duty would be a serious dereliction of
his prophetic mission:

O Messenger, deliver
that which has been sent down to you from your Lord;
for if you do not,
you will not have delivered His message. (5 : 70)

In perfect obedience to this command, the Holy Prophet, may Allah
bless him and grant him peace, from the moment he received the first
revelation right up until the last minutes of his life in this world, a
period of twenty-three years, bore untold hardships and waged an
unceasing struggle to fulfil the momentous duty entrusted to him.
Though his long and heroic struggle passed through many phases which
caused him to take on increasingly diverse roles for the fulfilment of his

mission, the Qur'an remained all along the pivotal point of all his activities. He was constantly occupied with reciting it, explaining its meaning, and communicating its message to the people.

The Holy Prophet's function of imparting the knowledge of the Book to the people, to enlighten and purify them, is described in four separate places in the Qur'an in exactly the same words:
**...to recite His signs to them and to purify them
and to teach them the Book and the Wisdom...**
These words indicate the technique we have suggested in the foregoing pages and at the same time explain the right method of bringing about the Islamic revolution in our society. By pursuing this method with extraordinary courage and determination for twenty-three years, the Holy Prophet acquitted himself faultlessly and conveyed God's message to mankind. He also sought the co-operation of his Companions in this task exhorting them to convey to others what he said even to the extent of a single *ayat*.

Having accomplished his mission, he transferred the responsibility of propagating the message of the Qur'an to his *umma*. On more than one occasion he obtained the testimony of the people to the effect that he had indeed conveyed God's message to them, and in his historic address to a gathering of one hundred and twenty-five thousand Companions during the Last Pilgrimmage he issued the following abiding instruction: *"Those who are present should convey to those who are absent."* Thus the duty of spreading God's message to every corner of the world devolved onto the shoulders of the Muslim nation for all time, and all the Muslims are answerable to the Almighty with regard to the discharge of this onerous duty. Since the Muslim nation consists of individuals, every individual is responsible for spreading the message of the Qur'an - men of learning according to their knowledge and ability and ordinary people according to their means and capacity.

The words of the Prophet: *"Convey from me to the people though it be a single ayat,"* prove beyond the shadow of a doubt that no individual is exempt from this duty. If a person can do nothing other than read the Arabic text of the Qur'an he should teach others to do that. If he has memorised the whole Qur'an he should help others to do the same. If he can translate the text of the Qur'an he should do that for others. And if he can comprehend its meaning he should explain and interpret it to others. If someone understands the meaning of one, single *sura* and explains it to others, or even if he only knows a single *ayat* and explains that, he will have discharged his duty of conveying the Qur'an to others. But the collective duty of the Muslim *umma* will not be fulfilled until the teaching of the Qur'an, both its text and its meaning, is propagated throughout the length and breadth of the world.

Unfortunately, in the present situation, this universal proclamation of God's message, which is expected of the Muslims as a whole, seems to be a far cry and an unattainable ideal, because things have come to such a pass that the *umma* to which this great duty was assigned has grown totally ignorant of the Qur'an and itself needs to be instructed in the Book of Allah which it has to all intents and purposes forsaken. Hence what is urgently required in the current situation is the launching of a movement for learning and teaching the Qur'an among the Muslims themselves, so that they can develop a fresh attitude of devotion to, and interest in, the study of the Qur'an. May God grant us strength for this task!

As was pointed out at the beginning of this discussion, a higher form of *tabligh* (communication) is *tabyin* (exposition). The message of the Qur'an is not only to be communicated, but its meaning must also be explained and interpreted to the people. In Qur'anic terminology, this has been called *tabyin*. Hence *tabligh* and *tabyin* appear together in the title of this chapter. The exposition of the Qur'an demands that the one who undertakes this task should talk to his audience at their own level so that the truths of the Qur'an are brought home to them and that he should also explain the implications and arguments of different *ayats* and *suras*.

It will be noted that the Qur'an calls itself *Bayan* (a plain statement):
> **This is a plain statement to men, a guidance**
> **and instruction to those who fear God. (3: 138)**

It frequently characterises itself as *mubin* (clear), and its verses as *bayyinat* and *mubayyinat* (clear signs or manifestations). It also points out that to explain and interpret the scriptures is the responsibility of the Prophets and the nations to whom they are sent. The Holy Prophet is addressed on this point in the following words:
> **And We have sent down unto you the message**
> **that you may explain clearly to men**
> **what has been sent down to them. (16: 44)**

It is stated that the Jews and Christians were bound by a covenant to explain the Book of God to mankind:

And remember God made a covenant
with the People of the Book:
'You should make it clear to the people.' (3 : 187)

When they did not fulfil this covenant and on the contrary tried to conceal the truth, they brought down a curse upon themselves:

Those who conceal the clear signs and guidance
We have sent down, after We have made it clear
for people in the Book,
on them shall rest of the curse of God
and the curse of those who curse. (2 : 159)

Tabyin has different forms. Its simplest form consists of expressing the plain meaning of the Qur'an in an easy, straightforward manner in the common language of the people. Naturally, the medium to be used for explaining the Qur'an to the people has to be their own language.

We sent not a messenger except (to teach)
in the language of his own people,
in order to make things clear to them. (14 : 4)

In its highest form, *tabyin* is a task with a challenge. Someone who resolves to fulfil the duty of explaining the Qur'an in this sense of the term will not merely translate its text, but attempt to unfold the knowledge and wisdom which this great book contains and bring out the implied meaning and subtle significance of its *ayats* and *suras*. He will explain the mode of inference and deduction used in the Qur'an and with the assistance of Qur'anic argument, effectively repudiate the false ideas and misleading opinions prevalent among people. He will endeavour to establish the truth of the Qur'an and its teachings, using a convincing form of reason at the highest level of thought accessible to the people concerned and compatible with their intellectual level.

Regarding how we can discharge our responsibility of explaining the Qur'an and bringing its message home to the people, we can say that for *tabyin* in its simplest form we should publish translations and commentaries of the Holy Book in all the major languages of the world and circulate them widely.

As far as our obligation for *tabyin* in its highest form is concerned, it cannot be properly and adequately discharged, as we have already said, unless we set up a network of universities all over the Muslim world where academics can concentrate on their studies and research on Qur'an, assigning to it the central place in the syllabus of their disciplines. By means of institutions of this type we shall be able to explain the teachings of the Qur'an to the people of the modern world.

6
POSTFACE
A direct word to the reader

Dear reader, excuse me for taking the liberty of addressing a few words to you directly. I am led to make this personal approach to you because of my great concern for your real welfare.

I have given you an idea of the duties which we as Muslims owe to the Qur'an and finally I must urge you as strongly as I can to make an earnest effort to discharge these duties with the utmost diligence. In that we possess the Book of Allah perfectly intact in its original form, we are the most fortunate people in the world . While it is a source of great honour for us, it also lays on us a heavy responsibility .

Prior to the advent of Islam, the Israelites were the custodians of God's Book, but when they did not discharge their responsibilities and proved unworthy of the honour bestowed on them, God Almighty raised a new *ummah* (i.e. the Muslims) and vouchsafed His Book to them in the form of the Qur'an. In *sura* 52 the likeness of the people who did not fulfil the duties that devolved upon them in their role as custodians of God's Book is given:

The likeness of those
who were charged with the Torah
but failed to carry it out,
is the likeness of a donkey bearing books. (52 : 5)

In the subsequent part of this verse, it is clearly stated that their failure to discharge their obligations towards their Holy Book is tantamount to falsifying its truth:

Evil is the likeness of the people
who falsify the signs of God. (52 : 5)

The verse ends with the categorical declaration that it is not in God's nature to grant guidance to such people:

And God does not guide people who do wrong. (52 : 5)

God forbid that you or I be included among the people who are guilty of falsifying the Book of God by their negligence in the discharge of their obligations towards it, thereby incurring His wrath. I most earnestly pray that God makes us custodians of the Qur'an in the true meaning of the term and enables us to fulfil our duties towards it in the best possible manner, thus enabling us to win His good pleasure.

We should remember the time when Allah's Messenger will appear as a witness for the prosecution in the court of the Almighty and charge his people with forsaking the Qur'an:

Then the Messenger will say:
'O my Lord! My people took this Qur'an
for just foolish nonsense...' (25 : 26)

Although in this *ayat* the words "my people" refer to the unbelievers, who turned a deaf ear to the Qur'an and treated it with disdain, it nevertheless applies equally well to people like us who believe in the Qur'an but treat it as a thing of no consequence.

Maulana Shabbir Ahmad 'Uthmani says concerning this: "Although this *ayat* actually refers to the unbelievers, all those who do not confirm the truth of the Qur'an by actually following its teachings during their lifetime, do not truly ponder its meanings, do not recite it properly, and do not attempt to learn its correct reading, but instead indulge in all sorts of vain and frivolous pursuits and turn their backs on it, also come under its scope and are guilty of *hijran al-Qur'an* (abandonment of the Qur'an)."

Let me once again seek the protection of the Almighty against our being included among such people, and conclude my address with the following prayer which is generally offered on the concluding the recitation of the entire Qur'an. I, however, believe that it should be offered frequently so that Allah will grant us the strength to fulfil the duties we owe His Book.

"O my Lord! Have mercy on us because of (our link) with the Qur'an! Make it our guide and a source of light, guidance and mercy for us! Make us remember what we have failed to understand of it. Give us the strength to recite it day and night. Make it a plea for our salvation, O Lord of the universe!"

Finally, let me present you with the gift of a prayer which appears in a tradition narrated on the authority of 'Abdullah b. Mas'ud. It is in fact a prayer which the Holy Prophet prescribed for his *Sahaba* as a remedy for cares and anxieties. But it is a splendid supplication that shows the attitude of an ideal slave towards his Master and describes the curative effect which the Qur'an has on the human soul. It also indicates the deep devotion which the Holy Prophet had to the Qur'an and the great esteem in which he held it. The prayer runs as follows:

42

'O my God! Truly I am Your slave, the son of Your slave and the son of Your slave-woman. I am under Your control. My forelock is in Your hand. Your decision about me is carried out and so shall Your judgment regarding me be carried out. I beg of You - addressing You with those names with which You have named Yourself, or which You have taught to any of Your creatures, or which You have revealed in Your Book, or which You have preferred to keep secret in the realm of the Unseen - to make the Qur'an a source of delight for my heart and of light for my breast, and an instrument for dispelling my grief, and driving away my cares and anxieties. Accept this prayer of mine, O Lord of the Universe!'

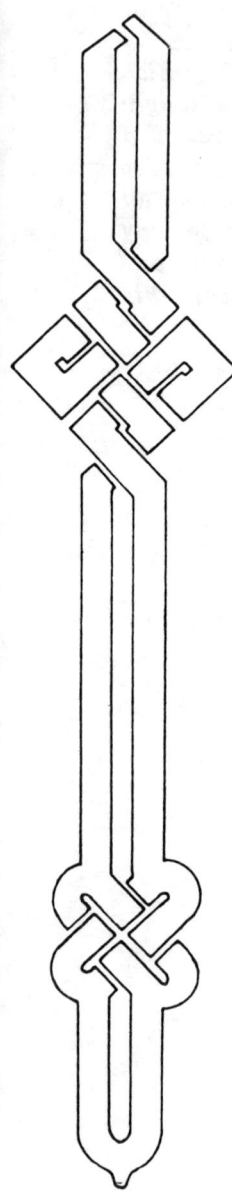

ISLAMIC
RENAISSANCE
THE REAL TASK AHEAD

DR. ISRAR AHMAD

RISE and DECLINE

of the

MUSLIM UMMAH

WITH A COMPARISON TO JEWISH HISTORY
AND A BRIEF SURVEY
OF THE PRESENT

EFFORTS TOWARDS AN
ISLAMIC RESURGENCE

●

Original in Urdu by:
DR. ISRAR AHMAD

●

Translated by:
DR. SANAULLAH ANSARI

Published by
Ta-Ha Publishers Ltd.
1, Wynne Road
LONDON SW9 0BD

THE QURĀN
AND WORLD PEACE

Original in Urdu by:
DR. ISRAR AHMAD

Translated by:
DR. ABSAR AHMAD

Ta-Ha Publishers Ltd
1, Wynne Rd London SW9 0BB